Easy Low-Calorie High-Protein Recipe Cookbook

Delicious, Original Meal Ideas with Vibrant Photos

By Steve Kemp

Copyright © 2023 By Steve Kemp

Introduction

Welcome to the Easy **Low-Calorie High-Protein Recipe Cookbook,** where health meets taste in a spectacular fusion of delicious, original meal ideas complemented by vibrant photographic images. Crafted with care by Steve Kemp, this culinary collection is designed to inspire and guide you through preparing nutritious meals that don't sacrifice flavor for fitness.

Are you tired of the same old diet routine? Looking for a way to invigorate your meals without piling on the calories? Your journey towards a healthier, more flavorful life begins here. This cookbook is your gateway to exploring a world where every recipe blends low-calorie content and high-protein benefits, perfect for fueling your body and satisfying your palate.

Imagine diving into a plateful of culinary delights that keep your health goals on track. From the succulence of perfectly cooked meats to the fresh zest of garden-picked vegetables, each recipe in this book is an original creation designed to delight your taste buds and boost your nutrition. Accompanied by stunning photos, these meals are as pleasing to the eye as they are to the palate.

Whether you're a seasoned chef or a novice in the kitchen, this cookbook provides easy-to-follow instructions and practical tips to ensure success. The variety of recipes ensures you'll find something to love, regardless of your dietary preferences or cooking skills. The vivid images inspire you, and the delicious outcomes motivate your culinary journey.

Embark on a flavorful adventure with the **Easy Low-Calorie High-Protein Recipe Cookbook.** Bring excitement back to your meals, nourish your body, and enjoy the process of cooking and eating well. Steve Kemp invites you to turn these pages, cook these recipes, and transform your diet into a delightful exploration of taste and health. Available now in Kindle & Paperback, this is your first step towards a happier, healthier you.

Table of Contents

Chapter 01 : Power Start Breakfasts

Recipe 01 : Spinach Avocado and Boiled Egg

Experience the perfect blend of health and flavor with Spinach, Avocado, and Boiled Egg salad. This delightful dish combines the nutritional powerhouses of spinach, avocado, and eggs, making it an ideal choice for a low-calorie, high-protein, satisfying, and delicious meal.

Servings: 2

Prepping Time: 10 minutes

Cook Time: 10 minutes

Difficulty: Easy

Ingredients:

- ✓ 2 cups fresh spinach leaves
- ✓ 1 ripe avocado, sliced
- ✓ 2 large eggs, hard-boiled and sliced
- ✓ 1 tablespoon olive oil
- ✓ 1 teaspoon lemon juice
- ✓ Salt and pepper, to taste
- ✓ Optional garnish: chia seeds or flax seeds

Step-by-Step Preparation:

1. Wash and dry the spinach leaves, then place them in a serving bowl.
2. Peel and slice the avocado, adding it to the bowl with spinach.
3. Slice the boiled eggs and arrange them over the spinach and avocado.
4. Whisk together olive oil, lemon juice, salt, and pepper in a small bowl. Drizzle this dressing over the salad.
5. Optionally, sprinkle chia seeds or flax seeds on top for added nutrition.

Nutritional Facts: (Per serving)

- ✓ Calories: 230
- ✓ Protein: 10g
- ✓ Carbohydrates: 8g
- ✓ Fat: 19g
- ✓ Dietary Fiber: 6g
- ✓ Sugars: 1g

Conclude your meal with this Spinach Avocado and Boiled Egg salad, a dish that guarantees a boost of energy and health. It's a simple, quick-to-prepare recipe perfect for those busy days when you want a nutritious meal without spending much time in the kitchen.

Recipe 02 : Crunchy Granola With Yogurt, Nuts

Discover the perfect start to your day with our Crunchy Granola with Yogurt and Nuts recipe. This dish, bursting with the goodness of whole grains and nuts, offers a nutritious, low-calorie, and high-protein meal that's as delicious as it is healthy.

Servings: 2

Prepping Time: 15 minutes

Cook Time: 0 minutes

Difficulty: Easy

Ingredients:

- ✓ 1 cup low-fat Greek yogurt
- ✓ 1/2 cup homemade or store-bought granola
- ✓ 1/4 cup mixed nuts (almonds, walnuts, pecans), chopped
- ✓ 1 tablespoon honey
- ✓ 1/2 teaspoon ground cinnamon
- ✓ Fresh fruits for topping (optional)

Step-by-Step Preparation:

1. Spoon the Greek yogurt into two bowls.
2. Sprinkle the granola evenly over the yogurt.
3. Add the chopped nuts on top of the granola.
4. Drizzle honey over the mixture and sprinkle with ground cinnamon.
5. Add fresh fruits on top for extra flavor and nutrients (optional).

Nutritional Facts: (Per serving)

- ✓ Calories: 280
- ✓ Protein: 17g
- ✓ Fat: 10g
- ✓ Carbohydrates: 36g
- ✓ Fiber: 4g
- ✓ Sugar: 22g

Conclude your morning ritual with this Crunchy Granola with Yogurt and Nuts, a delightful combination that energizes and satisfies you. It's an ideal recipe for health-conscious individuals seeking a quick, nutritious, delicious breakfast or snack.

Recipe 03 : Omelet With Salmon, Broccoli and Spinach

Step into a world of wholesome flavor with our Omelette with Salmon, Broccoli, and Spinach recipe. This delightful dish is a treat to your taste buds and a boon to your health, offering a perfect balance of low calories and high protein.

Servings: 2

Prepping Time: 10 minutes

Cook Time: 15 minutes

Difficulty: Medium

Ingredients:

- ✓ 4 large eggs
- ✓ 4 oz smoked salmon, thinly sliced
- ✓ 1 cup fresh spinach, chopped
- ✓ 1/2 cup broccoli florets, finely chopped
- ✓ 2 tablespoons milk
- ✓ 1 tablespoon olive oil
- ✓ Salt and pepper, to taste
- ✓ Fresh dill for garnish (optional)

Step-by-Step Preparation:

1. Beat the eggs with milk, salt, and pepper in a bowl.
2. Heat olive oil in a non-stick pan over medium heat.
3. Sauté the broccoli for 3-4 minutes until tender.
4. Add spinach and cook until wilted.
5. Pour the egg mixture over the vegetables, and cook for a few minutes until the bottom sets.
6. Lay the smoked salmon slices on one half of the omelet.
7. Gently fold the omelet in half, covering the salmon.
8. Cook for another 2-3 minutes until fully set.
9. Garnish with fresh dill if desired.

Nutritional Facts: (Per serving)

- ✓ Calories: 280
- • Protein: 23g
- • Fat: 18g
- • Carbohydrates: 4g
- • Fiber: 1g
- • Cholesterol: 372mg

Indulge in the rich and savory flavors of our Omelette with Salmon, Broccoli, and Spinach. It's a culinary masterpiece that combines nutrition and taste, making it an ideal meal for those seeking a healthy, protein-packed start to their day or a fulfilling, low-calorie lunch option.

Recipe 04 : Chia Pudding With Coconut Granola, Peanut Butter

Dive into a delightful fusion of taste and nutrition with our Chia Pudding with Coconut Granola and Peanut Butter recipe. This dish is a powerhouse of health benefits, offering a delicious blend of low-calorie and high-protein ingredients that are as satisfying as they are nourishing.

Servings: 2

Prepping Time: 15 minutes (plus overnight soaking)

Cook Time: 0 minutes

Difficulty: Easy

Ingredients:

- ✓ 1/4 cup chia seeds
- ✓ 1 cup almond milk
- ✓ 2 tablespoons peanut butter
- ✓ 1/2 cup coconut granola
- ✓ 1 tablespoon honey or maple syrup
- ✓ 1/2 teaspoon vanilla extract
- ✓ Fresh berries for topping (optional)

Step-by-Step Preparation:

1. In a bowl, mix chia seeds with almond milk and vanilla extract. Stir well.
2. Cover the mixture and refrigerate overnight, allowing the chia seeds to swell and form a pudding.
3. The following day, give the chia pudding a good stir. If it's too thick, add a little more almond milk.
4. Layer the chia pudding with peanut butter and coconut granola in serving bowls.
5. Drizzle with honey or maple syrup.
6. Top with fresh berries if desired.

Nutritional Facts: (Per serving)

- ✓ Calories: 315
- ✓ Protein: 10g
- ✓ Fat: 18g
- ✓ Carbohydrates: 30g
- ✓ Fiber: 9g
- ✓ Sugar: 10g

Savor each spoonful of this Chia Pudding with Coconut Granola and Peanut Butter, a recipe that's a perfect blend of health and flavor. Whether you're starting your day or looking for a nutritious snack, this dish is an ideal choice for those conscious about their health and palate.

Recipe 05 : Blueberry Muffin

Savor the goodness of Blueberry Muffins, a delightful treat that marries the sweetness of blueberries with the benefits of a low-calorie, high-protein recipe. Perfect for breakfast or a snack, these muffins will satisfy your cravings while keeping your health goals in check.

Servings: 12

Prepping Time: 15 minutes

Cook Time: 20 minutes

Difficulty: Medium

Ingredients:

- ✓ 1 ½ cups whole wheat flour
- ✓ ¾ cup vanilla protein powder
- ✓ 1 teaspoon baking powder
- ✓ ½ teaspoon baking soda
- ✓ ¼ teaspoon salt
- ✓ 2 large eggs
- ✓ ½ cup Greek yogurt
- ✓ ¼ cup honey
- ✓ ¼ cup almond milk
- ✓ 1 teaspoon vanilla extract
- ✓ 1 cup fresh blueberries

Step-by-Step Preparation:

1. Preheat your oven to 350°F (175°C) and line a muffin tin with paper liners.
2. Mix flour, protein powder, baking powder, baking soda, and salt in a bowl.
3. In another bowl, whisk eggs, Greek yogurt, honey, almond milk, and vanilla extract until smooth.
4. Combine the wet and dry ingredients and gently fold in the blueberries.
5. Distribute the batter evenly into the muffin tin and bake for 20 minutes or until a toothpick comes out clean.

Nutritional Facts: (Per serving)

- ✓ Calories: 120
- ✓ Protein: 8g
- ✓ Carbohydrates: 15g
- ✓ Fat: 3g
- ✓ Dietary Fiber: 2g
- ✓ Sugars: 7g

Enjoy these Blueberry Muffins as a healthy start to your day or a delightful afternoon snack. They're the perfect combination of tasty and nutritious, providing a guilt-free way to indulge in a baked favorite. Ideal for fitness enthusiasts and anyone seeking a healthier alternative to classic treats.

Chapter 02: Midday Fuel

Recipe 01 : Salad Chicken Pieces Cherry Tomatoe

Embark on a culinary journey with our Salad Chicken Pieces & Cherry Tomato recipe, a delightful blend of juicy chicken and fresh cherry tomatoes. Perfect for those seeking a nutritious yet delicious meal, it's a low-calorie, high-protein option that's both satisfying and easy to prepare.

Servings: 4

Prepping Time: 15 mins

Cook Time: 10 mins

Difficulty: Easy

Ingredients:

- ✓ 400g chicken breast, cut into pieces
- ✓ 200g cherry tomatoes, halved
- ✓ 1 large avocado, sliced
- ✓ 100g mixed salad leaves
- ✓ 2 tbsp olive oil
- ✓ 1 lemon, juiced
- ✓ 1 garlic clove, minced
- ✓ Salt and pepper to taste

Step-by-Step Preparation:

1. Season chicken with salt, pepper, and minced garlic.
2. Heat olive oil in a skillet and cook chicken until browned and cooked through.
3. Mix salad leaves, cherry tomatoes, and avocado in a large bowl.
4. Add the cooked chicken to the salad.
5. Drizzle with lemon juice and toss well.

Nutritional Facts: (Per serving)

- ✓ Calories: 250
- ✓ Protein: 26g
- ✓ Fat: 13g
- ✓ Carbohydrates: 8g
- ✓ Fiber: 4g

Finish your day with this vibrant Salad Chicken Pieces & Cherry Tomato dish, a perfect harmony of taste and nutrition. Ideal for a light lunch or a wholesome dinner, it's a recipe that promises satisfaction without compromising on health.

Recipe 02 : Homemade Avocado Tuna Wraps

Delight in the wholesome goodness of Homemade Avocado Tuna Wraps, a perfect blend of creamy avocado and nutritious tuna packed in a convenient wrap. This recipe is a testament to simplicity and health, offering a low-calorie, high-protein meal that's both quick to prepare and deliciously satisfying for any time of the day.

Servings: 4

Prepping Time: 10 mins

Cook Time: 0 mins

Difficulty: Easy

Ingredients:

- ✓ 2 cans of light tuna, drained
- ✓ 2 ripe avocados
- ✓ 1/2 red onion, finely chopped
- ✓ 2 tablespoons Greek yogurt
- ✓ 1 tablespoon lime juice
- ✓ 4 whole grain tortillas
- ✓ Salt and pepper, to taste
- ✓ Optional: mixed greens or spinach

Step-by-Step Preparation:

1. In a bowl, mash the avocados and mix with lime juice, Greek yogurt, salt, and pepper.
2. Fold in the tuna and red onion until well combined.
3. Spread the mixture over the tortillas.
4. Add mixed greens or spinach if desired.
5. Roll the tortillas tightly, cut in half, and serve.

Nutritional Facts: (Per serving)

- ✓ Calories: 280
- ✓ Protein: 25g
- ✓ Carbohydrates: 29g
- ✓ Fat: 9g
- ✓ Fiber: 6g

Enjoy the delightful and nutritious Homemade Avocado Tuna Wraps, a perfect meal for those on the go or looking for a quick and healthy option. Ideal for lunch, dinner, or a snack, these wraps are a great way to keep your diet on track while enjoying every bite.

Recipe 03 : Chicken or Turkey Roulade

Indulge in the savory delight of Chicken or Turkey Roulade, a dish that elegantly combines flavor and nutrition. Perfect for health-conscious food lovers, this recipe is a testament to how low-calorie, high-protein meals can be both delicious and sophisticated. With its tender meat and rich filling, the roulade offers a gourmet experience that's surprisingly simple to create at home.

Servings: 4

Prepping Time: 20 mins

Cook Time: 35 mins

Difficulty: Moderate

Ingredients:

- ✓ 4 chicken or turkey breast fillets
- ✓ 1/2 cup finely chopped spinach
- ✓ 1/4 cup finely chopped mushrooms
- ✓ 2 tablespoons low-fat cream cheese
- ✓ 1 teaspoon Dijon mustard
- ✓ Salt and pepper, to taste
- ✓ 1 tablespoon olive oil
- ✓ 1/2 teaspoon paprika

Step-by-Step Preparation:

1. Pound the chicken or turkey fillets to even thickness.
2. Mix spinach, mushrooms, cream cheese, mustard, salt, and pepper in a bowl.
3. Spread the filling over each fillet, roll tightly, and secure with toothpicks.
4. Rub the roulades with olive oil and paprika.
5. Bake in a preheated oven at 375°F (190°C) for 30-35 minutes.

Nutritional Facts: (Per serving)

- ✓ Calories: 230
- ✓ Protein: 35g
- ✓ Fat: 7g
- ✓ Carbohydrates: 4g
- ✓ Fiber: 1g

Conclude your day with the exquisite taste of Chicken or Turkey Roulade, a dish that brings a touch of gourmet to your dining table without compromising your health goals. This recipe is ideal for a special occasion or a nutritious family meal, proving that eating well can be elegant and effortless.

Recipe 04 : Shrimp Scampi With Lemon, Garlic, Butter and Herbs

Delve into the flavorful world of Shrimp Scampi with Lemon, Garlic, Butter, and Herbs, a dish that promises zesty and aromatic flavors in every bite. This recipe is a seafood lover's delight, offering a perfect balance of low-calorie, high-protein nutrition. It's an ideal choice for a quick yet elegant meal that's sure to impress.

Servings: 4

Prepping Time: 10 mins

Cook Time: 10 mins

Difficulty: Easy

Ingredients:

- ✓ 400g large shrimp, peeled and deveined
- ✓ 3 tablespoons unsalted butter
- ✓ 4 garlic cloves, minced
- ✓ 1/2 cup chicken or vegetable broth
- ✓ Juice of 1 lemon
- ✓ 2 tablespoons chopped fresh parsley
- ✓ 1 teaspoon red pepper flakes
- ✓ Salt and pepper to taste
- ✓ 1 tablespoon olive oil

Step-by-Step Preparation:

1. Heat olive oil and 1 tablespoon of butter in a skillet over medium heat.
2. Add garlic and red pepper flakes, sautéing for about 1 minute.
3. Increase the heat, add shrimp, and cook until they turn pink.
4. Pour in broth and lemon juice, simmering for 2 minutes.
5. Stir in the remaining butter, parsley, salt, and pepper.
6. Serve hot, garnished with extra parsley if desired.

Nutritional Facts: (Per serving)

- Calories: 180
- Protein: 23g
- Fat: 8g
- Carbohydrates: 2g
- Fiber: 0g

Conclude your day with the delightful Shrimp Scampi with Lemon, Garlic, Butter, and Herbs, combining simplicity with gourmet flavors. Whether it's a cozy family dinner or a special occasion, this recipe brings a touch of sophistication to your table while keeping your health and well-being in mind.

Recipe 05 : Fried Beef Stroganoff With Potatoes, Broccoli, Corn, Pepper, Carrots and Sauce

Embark on a culinary adventure with Fried Beef Stroganoff, a dish that artfully combines succulent beef with a medley of vibrant vegetables like potatoes, broccoli, corn, peppers, and carrots. Drizzled with a savory sauce, this low-calorie, high-protein recipe is a reimagined classic that's both nourishing and delightfully satisfying, perfect for those who cherish hearty, wholesome meals.

Servings: 4

Prepping Time: 15 mins

Cook Time: 30 mins

Difficulty: Moderate

Ingredients:

- ✓ 400g lean beef, sliced into strips
- ✓ 2 medium potatoes, cubed
- ✓ 1 cup broccoli florets
- ✓ 1/2 cup corn kernels
- ✓ 1 bell pepper, sliced
- ✓ 2 carrots, sliced
- ✓ 2 tablespoons olive oil
- ✓ 1 onion, chopped
- ✓ 2 garlic cloves, minced
- ✓ 1 cup beef broth
- ✓ 1 tablespoon Worcestershire sauce
- ✓ Salt and pepper to taste
- ✓ 1 tablespoon cornstarch (optional for thickening)

Step-by-Step Preparation:

1. Heat 1 tablespoon olive oil in a pan and fry the beef strips until browned. Set aside.
2. Add the remaining oil and sauté onion and garlic in the same pan.
3. Add potatoes, carrots, broccoli, bell pepper, and corn. Cook until vegetables are tender.
4. Return beef to the pan and add broth, Worcestershire sauce, salt, and pepper.
5. Simmer for 10 minutes. If desired, thicken the sauce with cornstarch mixed in water.
6. Serve hot.

Nutritional Facts: (Per serving)

- ✓ Calories: 320
- ✓ Protein: 25g
- ✓ Fat: 12g
- ✓ Carbohydrates: 30g
- ✓ Fiber: 5g

End your day on a high note with this flavorful Fried Beef Stroganoff, a dish that brings comfort and nutrition to your dinner table. It's an ideal choice for those seeking a fulfilling meal that's as health-conscious as delicious, proving that you can have the best of both worlds.

Chapter 03: Energizing Snacks

Recipe 01 : Almond Butter Dip With Onions And Cilantro Sticks

Immerse yourself in the unique flavors of Almond Butter Dip with Onions and Cilantro Sticks, a creative and nutritious snack that's as tasty as healthy. This low-calorie, high-protein recipe is a delightful twist on traditional dips, combining almond butter's rich, nutty taste with the fresh zest of onions and cilantro, perfect for a light snack or a delicious starter.

Servings: 4

Prepping Time: 10 mins

Cook Time: 0 mins

Difficulty: Easy

Ingredients:

- ✓ 1/2 cup natural almond butter
- ✓ 1/4 cup finely chopped red onion
- ✓ 1/4 cup chopped cilantro
- ✓ 2 tablespoons lemon juice
- ✓ 1 garlic clove, minced
- ✓ Salt and pepper to taste
- ✓ Water for consistency (optional)
- ✓ Cilantro sticks for dipping

Step-by-Step Preparation:

1. Combine almond butter, red onion, cilantro, lemon juice, and minced garlic in a mixing bowl.
2. Season with salt and pepper to taste.
3. If needed, adjust the consistency with a bit of water to achieve a dip-like texture.
4. Chill in the refrigerator for about 30 minutes.
5. Serve with cilantro sticks for dipping.

Nutritional Facts: (Per serving)

- ✓ Calories: 160
- ✓ Protein: 6g
- ✓ Fat: 14g
- ✓ Carbohydrates: 6g
- ✓ Fiber: 3g

Wrap up your day with this delightful Almond Butter Dip with Onions and Cilantro Sticks, a perfect snack for those who value health and flavor. Whether entertaining guests or looking for a nutritious snack, this dip offers a unique and delicious way to enjoy healthy eating.

Recipe 02 : Keto Cheese Melts, Crisps or Crackers

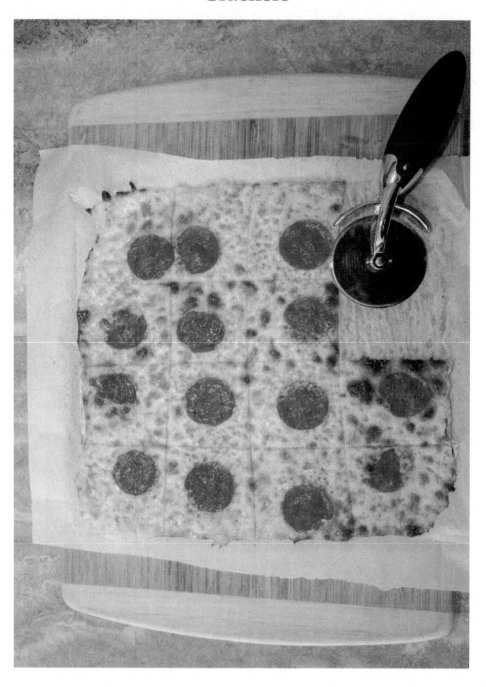

Indulge in the delightful crunch of Keto Cheese Melts, Crisps, or Crackers, a perfect snack for those following a keto diet or anyone looking for a low-calorie, high-protein treat. These cheesy delights are incredibly easy to make and offer the perfect blend of savoriness and crunch, ideal for satisfying your snack cravings without straying from your health goals.

Servings: 4

Prepping Time: 5 mins

Cook Time: 10 mins

Difficulty: Easy

Ingredients:

- ✓ 1 cup shredded mozzarella cheese
- ✓ 1 cup shredded cheddar cheese
- ✓ 1/2 teaspoon garlic powder
- ✓ 1/2 teaspoon paprika (optional)
- ✓ Parchment paper for baking

Step-by-Step Preparation:

1. Preheat your oven to 350°F (175°C).
2. Combine mozzarella and cheddar cheese in a bowl.
3. Mix in garlic powder and paprika.
4. Place parchment paper on a baking sheet.
5. Drop tiny heaps of the cheese mixture onto the sheet, flattening them slightly.
6. Bake for 8-10 minutes or until golden and crisp.
7. Let them cool before serving.

Nutritional Facts: (Per serving)

- ✓ Calories: 150
- ✓ Protein: 10g
- ✓ Fat: 12g
- ✓ Carbohydrates: 1g
- ✓ Fiber: 0g

End your day with these scrumptious Keto Cheese Melts, Crisps, or Crackers, a simple yet delicious way to stick to your keto goals. Whether you're after a quick snack or a tasty side for your salads and soups, these cheesy treats are a guilt-free pleasure you can enjoy any time.

Recipe 03 : Roast Butternut Squash and Chickpeas

Embrace autumn flavors any time with this Roast Butternut Squash and Chickpeas recipe. A delightful fusion of sweet, earthy squash and nutty chickpeas, this dish is a testament to the joys of simple, healthy cooking. Ideal for those seeking a low-calorie, high-protein meal, it's nutritious, incredibly satisfying, and flavorful.

Servings: 4

Prepping Time: 10 mins

Cook Time: 25 mins

Difficulty: Easy

Ingredients:

- ✓ 1 large butternut squash, peeled and diced
- ✓ 1 can (400g) chickpeas, drained and rinsed
- ✓ 2 tbsp olive oil
- ✓ 1 tsp ground cinnamon
- ✓ 1/2 tsp ground nutmeg
- ✓ Salt and pepper to taste
- ✓ 2 tbsp honey (optional for sweetness)

Step-by-Step Preparation:

1. Preheat your oven to 425°F (220°C).
2. Mix the butternut squash with olive oil, cinnamon, nutmeg, salt, and pepper in a large bowl.
3. Spread the squash on a baking tray in a single layer.
4. Roast for 15 minutes, then add chickpeas to the tray.
5. Drizzle honey over the mixture, if using, and roast for another 10 minutes or until the squash is tender.

Nutritional Facts: (Per serving)

- ✓ Calories: 220
- ✓ Protein: 5g
- ✓ Fat: 7g
- ✓ Carbohydrates: 35g
- ✓ Fiber: 6g

Relish the comforting and wholesome goodness of Roast Butternut Squash and Chickpeas. This dish is a superb way to enjoy a healthy, filling meal with flavor and nutritional benefits. Perfect for a family dinner or a comforting solo meal, it's a recipe that will leave you feeling satisfied and nourished.

Recipe 04 : Delicious Smoked Salmon and Olive Canapes

Savor the elegant flavors of Delicious Smoked Salmon and Olive Canapés, a gourmet appetizer that's simple to prepare and delightfully sophisticated. This low-calorie, high-protein recipe pairs the rich taste of smoked salmon with the tangy zest of olives, creating a perfect harmony of flavors. Ideal for gatherings, special occasions, or as a luxurious snack, these canapés are sure to impress and satisfy.

Servings: 6

Prepping Time: 20 mins

Cook Time: 0 mins

Difficulty: Easy

Ingredients:

- ✓ 150g smoked salmon, thinly sliced
- ✓ 1/2 cup cream cheese, light
- ✓ 2 tablespoons chopped fresh chives
- ✓ 1/4 cup green olives, finely chopped
- ✓ 1 teaspoon lemon zest
- ✓ Black pepper to taste
- ✓ 12 whole grain crackers
- ✓ Fresh dill for garnish

Step-by-Step Preparation:

1. Blend cream cheese with chives, olives, lemon zest, and black pepper in a bowl.
2. Spread a thin layer of the cream cheese mixture on each cracker.
3. Top each cracker with a slice of smoked salmon.
4. Garnish with a small sprig of dill.
5. Arrange on a platter and serve immediately.

Nutritional Facts: (Per serving)

- ✓ Calories: 90
- ✓ Protein: 6g
- ✓ Fat: 5g
- ✓ Carbohydrates: 7g
- ✓ Fiber: 1g

Enjoy the luxurious and delectable experience of Delicious Smoked Salmon and Olive Canapés, a perfect start to any meal or a classy addition to your appetizer spread. Their ease of preparation and exquisite taste make them a top choice for health-conscious gourmets seeking sophistication without the extra calories.

Recipe 05 : Cucumber, Smoked Tuna and Avocado Salad

Immerse yourself in the refreshing and nutritious world of Cucumber, Smoked Tuna, and Avocado Salad. This dish celebrates simple, natural flavors and textures, combining the crispness of cucumber, the richness of smoked tuna, and the creaminess of avocado. It's a low-calorie, high-protein salad perfect for a health-conscious lifestyle, offering a satisfying yet light dining experience.

Servings: 4

Prepping Time: 15 mins

Cook Time: 0 mins

Difficulty: Easy

Ingredients:

- ✓ 2 large cucumbers, thinly sliced
- ✓ 200g smoked tuna, flaked
- ✓ 1 ripe avocado, diced
- ✓ 1/4 red onion, thinly sliced
- ✓ 2 tablespoons lemon juice
- ✓ 2 tablespoons olive oil
- ✓ Salt and pepper to taste
- ✓ Fresh dill for garnish

Step-by-Step Preparation:

1. Combine the sliced cucumbers, smoked tuna, and diced avocado in a large bowl.

2. Add the thinly sliced red onion to the bowl.

3. Whisk together lemon juice, olive oil, salt, and pepper in a small bowl to create the dressing.

4. Pour the dressing over the salad and toss gently to coat.

5. Garnish with fresh dill before serving.

Nutritional Facts: (Per serving)

- ✓ Calories: 180
- ✓ Protein: 12g
- ✓ Fat: 12g
- ✓ Carbohydrates: 8g
- ✓ Fiber: 4g

Conclude your meal with this delightful Cucumber, Smoked Tuna, and Avocado Salad, a dish that's as pleasing to the palate as it is to the body. It's the perfect choice for a light lunch or dinner or as a healthy addition to your meal plan, embodying the essence of nutritious yet delicious eating.

Chapter 04: Protein-Rich Dinners

Recipe 01 : Grilled Chicken With Spice Rub and Lemon

Indulge in the savory delight of Grilled Chicken with Spice Rub and Lemon, a perfect blend of zest and spice. This low-calorie, high-protein dish is an ideal choice for health-conscious gourmets.

Servings: 4

Prepping Time: 15 minutes

Cook Time: 20 minutes

Difficulty: Easy

Ingredients:

- ✓ 4 boneless, skinless chicken breasts
- ✓ 2 tablespoons olive oil
- ✓ 1 teaspoon paprika
- ✓ 1 teaspoon garlic powder
- ✓ 1/2 teaspoon cayenne pepper
- ✓ Salt and black pepper to taste
- ✓ 1 lemon, thinly sliced

Step-by-Step Preparation:

1. Preheat the grill to medium-high heat.
2. Mix olive oil, paprika, garlic powder, cayenne pepper, salt, and black pepper in a bowl.
3. Coat the chicken breasts evenly with the spice mixture.
4. Place chicken on the grill and cook for 10 minutes on each side.
5. Add lemon slices on top in the last 5 minutes of grilling.

Nutritional Facts: (Per serving)

- ✓ Calories: 220
- ✓ Protein: 26g
- ✓ Fat: 10g
- ✓ Carbohydrates: 3g
- ✓ Sodium: 70mg

Savor the mouth-watering Grilled Chicken with Spice Rub and Lemon, a culinary masterpiece that promises a delightful and healthy dining experience. Its tantalizing flavors and easy preparation make it a must-try for all.

Recipe 02 : Beef and Broccoli Stir Fry

Dive into the savory world of Beef and Broccoli Stir Fry, a classic dish that marries the richness of beef with the freshness of broccoli. This low-calorie, high-protein recipe is a treat to your taste buds and a boon for your health, making it a perfect fit for any meal plan.

Servings: 4

Prepping Time: 15 minutes

Cook Time: 10 minutes

Difficulty: Easy

Ingredients:

- ✓ 500g lean beef, thinly sliced
- ✓ 3 cups broccoli, cut into florets
- ✓ 2 tablespoons soy sauce
- ✓ 1 tablespoon sesame oil
- ✓ 1 teaspoon garlic, minced
- ✓ 1 teaspoon ginger, grated
- ✓ 1 tablespoon cornstarch
- ✓ ½ cup water or beef stock
- ✓ Salt and pepper to taste

Step-by-Step Preparation:

1. Marinate beef in soy sauce, sesame oil, garlic, and ginger for 10 minutes.
2. In a skillet, stir-fry marinated beef over medium-high heat until browned. Remove and set aside.
3. In the same skillet, add broccoli and water or beef stock. Cover and cook until broccoli is tender.
4. Return beef to the skillet, add cornstarch slurry, and stir until the sauce thickens.

Nutritional Facts: (Per serving)

- ✓ Calories: 230
- ✓ Protein: 25g
- ✓ Fat: 8g
- ✓ Carbohydrates: 10g
- ✓ Sodium: 500mg

Enjoy the delightful Beef and Broccoli Stir Fry, a simple yet flavorful dish that will satisfy your cravings. Whether a quick weeknight dinner or a special weekend meal, this recipe promises everyone a delicious and nutritious experience.

Recipe 03 : Crispy Pork Chop, Mushroom Sauce and Creamy Mashed Potatoes

Savor the delightful combination of Crispy Pork Chop with Mushroom Sauce and Creamy Mashed Potatoes. This dish, a symphony of flavors, is a low-calorie, high-protein culinary masterpiece, perfect for those who love a hearty meal without compromising their health goals.

Servings: 4

Prepping Time: 20 minutes

Cook Time: 30 minutes

Difficulty: Moderate

Ingredients:

- ✓ 4 boneless pork chops
- ✓ 2 cups mushrooms, sliced
- ✓ 4 potatoes, peeled and cubed
- ✓ 1 cup low-fat milk
- ✓ 2 tablespoons olive oil
- ✓ 1 onion, finely chopped
- ✓ 2 garlic cloves, minced
- ✓ 1 tablespoon flour
- ✓ 1 cup chicken broth
- ✓ Salt and pepper to taste

Step-by-Step Preparation:

1. Boil potatoes until tender, and mash with low-fat milk, salt, and pepper.

2. Season pork chops with salt and pepper, then fry in olive oil until golden and crispy.

3. For the sauce, sauté onions and garlic, add mushrooms, and cook until soft.

4. Stir in flour, add chicken broth, and simmer until thickened.

Nutritional Facts: (Per serving)

- ✓ Calories: 350
- ✓ Protein: 30g
- ✓ Fat: 15g
- ✓ Carbohydrates: 25g
- ✓ Sodium: 300mg

Enjoy the perfect balance of taste and nutrition with Crispy Pork Chop, Mushroom Sauce, and Creamy Mashed Potatoes. It's a delightful dish that brings comfort and satisfaction to your dining table, ideal for a family dinner or a special occasion.

Recipe 04 : Garlic Chili Prawns Shrimps

Indulge in the tantalizing flavors of Garlic chili prawns, a sumptuous dish that's light and packed with protein. Perfect for seafood lovers, this recipe combines the zesty punch of garlic and chili with succulent prawns, creating a low-calorie yet high-protein feast that's sure to delight your palate.

Servings: 4

Prepping Time: 10 minutes

Cook Time: 10 minutes

Difficulty: Easy

Ingredients:

- ✓ 400g large prawns, shelled and deveined
- ✓ 3 garlic cloves, minced
- ✓ 1 red chilli, finely sliced
- ✓ 2 tablespoons olive oil
- ✓ Juice of 1 lemon
- ✓ Salt and pepper to taste
- ✓ Fresh parsley, chopped for garnish

Step-by-Step Preparation:

1. Heat olive oil in a pan over medium heat.
2. Add garlic and chili, and sauté until fragrant.
3. Toss in the prawns and cook until they turn pink and opaque.
4. Season with salt, pepper, and lemon juice.
5. Garnish with fresh parsley before serving.

Nutritional Facts: (Per serving)

- ✓ Calories: 120
- ✓ Protein: 23g
- ✓ Fat: 3g
- ✓ Carbohydrates: 2g
- ✓ Sodium: 300mg

Garlic Chilli Prawns is a perfect dish for those who desire a quick yet healthy and flavorful meal. Whether it's a weeknight dinner or a special occasion, this recipe will impress with its simplicity and bold flavors.

Recipe 05 : Homemade Spaghetti and Turkey Meatballs

Delve into the heartwarming world of Homemade Spaghetti and Turkey Meatballs, a classic dish reimagined with a healthier twist. This low-calorie, high-protein recipe brings the comfort of traditional Italian cuisine to your table, making it an ideal choice for those seeking a nourishing yet delicious meal.

Servings: 4

Prepping Time: 30 minutes

Cook Time: 30 minutes

Difficulty: Medium

Ingredients:

- ✓ 300g spaghetti
- ✓ 400g ground turkey
- ✓ 1 onion, finely chopped
- ✓ 2 garlic cloves, minced
- ✓ 1 egg
- ✓ 1/4 cup whole wheat breadcrumbs
- ✓ 2 cups tomato sauce
- ✓ 1 teaspoon dried oregano
- ✓ Salt and pepper to taste
- ✓ Fresh basil for garnish

Step-by-Step Preparation:

1. Cook spaghetti according to package instructions.
2. Combine ground turkey, onion, garlic, egg, breadcrumbs, salt, and pepper. Form into meatballs.
3. Brown meatballs in a pan, then add tomato sauce and oregano. Simmer for 20 minutes.
4. Serve meatballs over spaghetti, garnished with fresh basil.

Nutritional Facts: (Per serving)

- ✓ Calories: 350
- ✓ Protein: 28g
- ✓ Fat: 8g
- ✓ Carbohydrates: 44g
- ✓ Sodium: 500mg

Enjoy Homemade Spaghetti and Turkey Meatballs, a dish that's pleasing to the palate and kind to your health. It's a perfect blend of comfort and nourishment, ideal for a cozy family dinner or a special gathering with friends.

Chapter 05: Vegetarian Delights

Recipe 01 : Creamy Avocado and Spinach Pasta

Dive into the world of healthy indulgence with Creamy Avocado and Spinach Pasta. This recipe, combining the goodness of avocados and the freshness of spinach, creates a low-calorie, high-protein dish that is as nutritious as it is delicious. Perfect for health-conscious pasta lovers, it's a guilt-free meal that doesn't compromise on taste.

Servings: 4

Prepping Time: 15 minutes

Cook Time: 10 minutes

Difficulty: Easy

Ingredients:

- ✓ 200g whole wheat pasta
- ✓ 2 ripe avocados
- ✓ 2 cups fresh spinach
- ✓ 1 clove garlic
- ✓ Juice of 1 lemon
- ✓ 2 tablespoons olive oil
- ✓ Salt and pepper to taste
- ✓ Grated Parmesan cheese for garnish

Step-by-Step Preparation:

1. Cook pasta according to package instructions.
2. Blend avocados, spinach, garlic, lemon juice, and olive oil in a food processor until smooth.
3. Drain pasta and return to pot.
4. Mix in the avocado-spinach sauce and season with salt and pepper.
5. Serve garnished with Parmesan cheese.

Nutritional Facts: (Per serving)

- ✓ Calories: 320
- ✓ Protein: 10g
- ✓ Fat: 15g
- ✓ Carbohydrates: 40g
- ✓ Sodium: 60mg

Creamy Avocado and Spinach Pasta are perfect for a quick, healthy meal. Whether you need a speedy weeknight dinner or a nutritious lunch option, this dish will surely please everyone with its creamy texture and rich flavors.

Recipe 02 : Lentil Curry With Chickpeas, White Rice and Fresh Cilantro

Embark on a culinary journey with Lentil Curry with Chickpeas, White Rice, and Fresh Cilantro. This dish is a delightful blend of robust flavors and hearty ingredients, creating a low-calorie, high-protein meal that's both satisfying and nutritious. Perfect for those seeking a wholesome and flavorful dining experience, it's a testament to the rich and diverse world of plant-based cuisine.

Servings: 4

Prepping Time: 20 minutes

Cook Time: 35 minutes

Difficulty: Medium

Ingredients:

- ✓ 1 cup lentils
- ✓ 1 cup chickpeas, cooked
- ✓ 2 cups white rice
- ✓ 1 onion, chopped
- ✓ 2 garlic cloves, minced
- ✓ 1 tablespoon curry powder
- ✓ 1 teaspoon cumin
- ✓ 1 can (400ml) coconut milk
- ✓ 2 cups vegetable broth
- ✓ Salt and pepper to taste
- ✓ Fresh cilantro for garnish

Step-by-Step Preparation:

1. Cook rice according to package instructions.
2. Sauté onion and garlic until translucent.
3. Add lentils, chickpeas, curry powder, and cumin; cook for 2 minutes.
4. Pour in coconut milk and vegetable broth; simmer until lentils are tender.
5. Season with salt and pepper.
6. Serve the curry over rice garnished with fresh cilantro.

Nutritional Facts: (Per serving)

- ✓ Calories: 350
- ✓ Protein: 18g
- ✓ Fat: 9g
- ✓ Carbohydrates: 55g
- ✓ Sodium: 300mg

Lentil Curry with Chickpeas, White Rice, and Fresh Cilantro is a perfect meal for those who love to explore diverse flavors while maintaining a health-conscious diet. It's a dish that feeds the body and delights the senses, ideal for a cozy family dinner or a special gathering.

Recipe 03 : Stuffed Pepper With Cauliflower and Tomato

Experience the delightful combination of flavors and textures in Stuffed Peppers with Cauliflower and Tomato, a culinary creation that's both low in calories and high in protein. This dish, featuring bell peppers stuffed with a savory mix of cauliflower and tomato, is a testament to how nutritious ingredients can come together deliciously and healthfully.

Servings: 4

Prepping Time: 15 minutes

Cook Time: 25 minutes

Difficulty: Easy

Ingredients:

- ✓ 4 large bell peppers, tops removed and seeded
- ✓ 2 cups cauliflower, finely chopped
- ✓ 1 cup cherry tomatoes, halved
- ✓ 1 onion, finely chopped
- ✓ 2 garlic cloves, minced
- ✓ 1 teaspoon dried oregano
- ✓ 2 tablespoons olive oil
- ✓ Salt and pepper to taste
- ✓ Fresh parsley for garnish

Step-by-Step Preparation:

1. Preheat oven to 375°F (190°C).
2. Sauté onion and garlic in olive oil until translucent.
3. Add cauliflower and cook for 5 minutes.
4. Stir in tomatoes, oregano, salt, and pepper.
5. Stuff the mixture into the bell peppers.
6. Place stuffed peppers in a baking dish and bake for 20 minutes.
7. Garnish with fresh parsley before serving.

Nutritional Facts: (Per serving)

- ✓ Calories: 150
- ✓ Protein: 4g
- ✓ Fat: 7g
- ✓ Carbohydrates: 20g
- ✓ Sodium: 50mg

Stuffed Pepper with Cauliflower and Tomato is perfect for those seeking a light yet satisfying dining experience. Its simple ingredients and robust flavors make it an excellent choice for a healthy lunch or dinner, ideal for casual meals and special occasions.

Recipe 04 : Garlic and Broccolis Stir Fried With Chickpeas

Dive into the world of vibrant flavors with Garlic and Broccoli Stir-Fried with Chickpeas. This dish is a powerhouse of nutrition, combining broccoli's crunch with chickpeas's heartiness, all brought together with a burst of garlic flavor. A perfect low-calorie, high-protein recipe that's easy to prepare and a delight to your taste buds.

Servings: 4

Prepping Time: 10 minutes

Cook Time: 15 minutes

Difficulty: Easy

Ingredients:

- ✓ 3 cups broccoli florets
- ✓ 1 can chickpeas, drained and rinsed
- ✓ 4 garlic cloves, minced
- ✓ 2 tablespoons olive oil
- ✓ 1 teaspoon soy sauce
- ✓ Salt and pepper to taste
- ✓ Red pepper flakes (optional)

Step-by-Step Preparation:

1. Heat olive oil in a pan over medium heat.
2. Add garlic and sauté until fragrant.
3. Toss in broccoli and stir-fry for about 5 minutes.
4. Add chickpeas, soy sauce, salt, and red pepper flakes.
5. Stir-fry for another 5-10 minutes until broccoli is tender but crisp.

Nutritional Facts: (Per serving)

- ✓ Calories: 190
- ✓ Protein: 9g
- ✓ Fat: 8g
- ✓ Carbohydrates: 24g
- ✓ Sodium: 300mg

Garlic and Broccoli Stir-Fried with Chickpeas is a beautiful dish for those seeking a quick, healthy, and flavorful meal. It's a fantastic way to incorporate more greens and protein into your diet, perfect for a light lunch or a wholesome dinner.

Recipe 05 : Thai Style Noodles , Pad Thai Pork

Embark on a culinary adventure with Thai Thai-style noodles and Pad Thai Pork - a dish that brings the essence of Thai street food right to your table. This recipe, combining the exotic flavors of Thailand with lean protein-rich pork, offers a low-calorie yet high-protein meal. It's perfect for anyone who enjoys a flavorful, nutritious, filling, and satisfying dish.

Servings: 4

Prepping Time: 20 minutes

Cook Time: 15 minutes

Difficulty: Medium

Ingredients:

- ✓ 200g rice noodles
- ✓ 300g lean pork, thinly sliced
- ✓ 2 eggs, lightly beaten
- ✓ 1 cup bean sprouts
- ✓ 1 carrot, julienned
- ✓ 3 green onions, chopped
- ✓ 2 tablespoons fish sauce
- ✓ 1 tablespoon tamarind paste
- ✓ 1 tablespoon brown sugar
- ✓ 2 cloves garlic, minced
- ✓ 1 lime, wedged for serving
- ✓ Crushed peanuts for garnish
- ✓ 2 tablespoons vegetable oil

Step-by-Step Preparation:

1. Soak rice noodles in warm water until soft.
2. Heat oil in a wok and fry garlic until fragrant.
3. Add pork and cook until browned.
4. Push pork to the side, add eggs, and scramble.
5. Add drained noodles, fish sauce, tamarind paste, and brown sugar.
6. Toss in carrots, bean sprouts, and green onions.
7. Stir-fry until everything is well mixed and heated through.

Nutritional Facts: (Per serving)

- ✓ Calories: 320
- ✓ Protein: 22g
- ✓ Fat: 10g
- ✓ Carbohydrates: 35g
- ✓ Sodium: 600mg

Thai Style Noodles: Pad Thai Pork is an ideal dish for those who love exploring international cuisine without leaving the comfort of their kitchen. It's a delicious way to bring a taste of Thailand into your healthy eating plan, perfect for a family dinner or a special occasion.

Chapter 06: Soupier Protein Boosts

Recipe 01 : Spicy White Chili Chicken With Vegetables

Delight in the flavors of Spicy White Chili Chicken with Vegetables, a dish that brings a zesty twist to your mealtime. This low-calorie, high-protein recipe is a fusion of tender chicken, various vegetables, and a kick of spice. It offers a nutritious yet compelling option for those who enjoy a little heat in their healthy meals.

Servings: 4

Prepping Time: 15 minutes

Cook Time: 30 minutes

Difficulty: Medium

Ingredients:

- ✓ 500g chicken breast, cubed
- ✓ 1 onion, diced
- ✓ 2 garlic cloves, minced
- ✓ 1 bell pepper, chopped
- ✓ 1 can white beans, drained and rinsed
- ✓ 1 can corn, drained
- ✓ 1 liter chicken broth
- ✓ 1 teaspoon cumin
- ✓ 1 teaspoon chili powder
- ✓ Salt and pepper to taste
- ✓ Fresh cilantro for garnish
- ✓ 1 tablespoon olive oil

Step-by-Step Preparation:

1. Heat olive oil in a pot and sauté onion and garlic until soft.
2. Add chicken and cook until browned.
3. Stir in bell pepper, white beans, corn, cumin, and chili powder.
4. Pour in chicken broth and bring to a boil.
5. Simmer for 20 minutes.
6. Season with salt and pepper.
7. Garnish with fresh cilantro before serving.

Nutritional Facts: (Per serving)

- ✓ Calories: 260
- ✓ Protein: 30g
- ✓ Fat: 6g
- ✓ Carbohydrates: 22g
- ✓ Sodium: 500mg

Spicy White Chili Chicken with Vegetables is perfect for those seeking a hearty and healthful dish. It's a great way to enjoy a protein-packed meal with the bonus of a flavorful, spicy broth, ideal for a cozy night in or a nutritious family dinner.

Recipe 02 : Vegetable Cream Soup With Shrimps and Croutons

Immerse yourself in the rich and creamy delight of Vegetable Cream Soup with Shrimp and Croutons. This exquisite dish combines the smoothness of blended vegetables with the juiciness of shrimp, topped with crunchy croutons. A low-calorie, high-protein choice, it's ideal for those who cherish sophisticated flavors while maintaining a health-conscious diet.

Servings: 4

Prepping Time: 20 minutes

Cook Time: 30 minutes

Difficulty: Medium

Ingredients:

- ✓ 200g shrimps, peeled and deveined
- ✓ 2 cups mixed vegetables (carrots, broccoli, cauliflower)
- ✓ 1 onion, chopped
- ✓ 2 garlic cloves, minced
- ✓ 4 cups vegetable broth
- ✓ 1 cup low-fat cream
- ✓ 1 tablespoon olive oil
- ✓ Salt and pepper to taste
- ✓ Homemade croutons for garnish

Step-by-Step Preparation:

1. In a pot, heat olive oil and sauté onion and garlic until translucent.
2. Add mixed vegetables and cook for 5 minutes.
3. Pour in vegetable broth and bring to a boil. Simmer until vegetables are soft.
4. Blend the mixture until smooth, and return to the pot.
5. Add cream and shrimps, and cook until shrimps are pink.
6. Season with salt and pepper.
7. Serve hot, garnished with croutons.

Nutritional Facts: (Per serving)

- ✓ Calories: 220
- ✓ Protein: 15g
- ✓ Fat: 8g
- ✓ Carbohydrates: 20g
- ✓ Sodium: 480mg

Vegetable Cream Soup with Shrimp and Croutons is an elegant, nourishing dish that perfectly combines health and flavor. Whether it's a sophisticated starter or a light main course, this soup will impress with its creamy texture and rich taste, making it a favorite for special occasions and everyday meals.

Recipe 03 : Hearty Hamburger Soup With Barley

Indulge in the comforting embrace of Hearty Hamburger Soup with Barley, a perfect blend of rich flavors and nourishing ingredients. This low-calorie, high-protein recipe is more than just a soup; it's a wholesome meal in a bowl. Packed with lean meat, hearty barley, and a medley of vegetables, it's designed to satisfy hunger and provide lasting energy.

Servings: 4

Prepping Time: 15 minutes

Cook Time: 45 minutes

Difficulty: Easy

Ingredients:

- ✓ 400g lean ground beef
- ✓ 1 cup barley, rinsed
- ✓ 1 onion, chopped
- ✓ 2 carrots, diced
- ✓ 2 celery stalks, diced
- ✓ 3 garlic cloves, minced
- ✓ 1 can diced tomatoes (400g)
- ✓ 4 cups beef broth
- ✓ 1 teaspoon dried thyme
- ✓ 1 teaspoon dried oregano
- ✓ Salt and pepper to taste
- ✓ 2 tablespoons olive oil

Step-by-Step Preparation:

1. In a large pot, heat olive oil and cook ground beef until browned.
2. Add onions, carrots, and celery; cook until softened.
3. Stir in garlic, thyme, and oregano; cook for another minute.
4. Add barley, diced tomatoes, and beef broth.
5. Bring to a boil, then reduce heat and simmer for 30-35 minutes until barley is tender.
6. Season with salt and pepper to taste.

Nutritional Facts: (Per serving)

- ✓ Calories: 350
- ✓ Protein: 25g
- ✓ Fat: 10g
- ✓ Carbohydrates: 40g
- ✓ Sodium: 500mg

Hearty Hamburger Soup with Barley is the epitome of comfort food, combining simplicity and nourishment. It's a versatile dish that's perfect for a cozy family dinner or a satisfying lunch, offering a delicious way to keep warm and energized during colder days.

Recipe 04 : Bowl of Tasty Lentils Soup

Discover the hearty and wholesome goodness of a Bowl of Tasty Lentil Soup. This simple yet flavorful recipe is a treasure trove of nutrition, offering a low-calorie, high-protein option for anyone seeking a comforting and satisfying meal. Packed with lentils and a blend of aromatic vegetables, it's a perfect choice for health-conscious individuals who don't want to compromise on taste.

Servings: 4

Prepping Time: 10 minutes

Cook Time: 30 minutes

Difficulty: Easy

Ingredients:

- ✓ 1 cup lentils, rinsed
- ✓ 1 large onion, chopped
- ✓ 2 carrots, diced
- ✓ 2 celery stalks, diced
- ✓ 3 garlic cloves, minced
- ✓ 4 cups vegetable broth
- ✓ 1 teaspoon ground cumin
- ✓ 1/2 teaspoon paprika
- ✓ Salt and pepper to taste
- ✓ 2 tablespoons olive oil
- ✓ Fresh parsley for garnish

Step-by-Step Preparation:

1. Heat olive oil in a large pot over medium heat.
2. Sauté onion, carrots, and celery until softened.
3. Add garlic, cumin, and paprika, and cook for another minute.
4. Stir in lentils and vegetable broth.
5. Bring to a boil, then reduce heat and simmer for 20-25 minutes until lentils are tender.
6. Season with salt and pepper.
7. Garnish with fresh parsley before serving.

Nutritional Facts: (Per serving)

- ✓ Calories: 200
- ✓ Protein: 14g
- ✓ Fat: 5g
- ✓ Carbohydrates: 30g
- ✓ Sodium: 300mg

A Bowl of Tasty Lentil Soup is not just a meal; it's a warm embrace in a bowl, ideal for those chilly evenings or as a nutritious lunch option. It's a testament to the power of simple ingredients to create something truly delightful and nourishing.

Recipe 05 : Creamy Soup With Salmon, Asparagus Beans

Delve into the luxurious taste of Creamy Soup with Salmon and Asparagus Beans, a dish that's as nourishing as it is delicious. This exquisite soup combines the rich flavors of salmon with the crisp freshness of asparagus beans, all enveloped in a creamy broth. A perfect choice for those seeking a low-calorie, high-protein meal, it's a culinary delight that's both satisfying and health-conscious.

Servings: 4

Prepping Time: 15 minutes

Cook Time: 25 minutes

Difficulty: Medium

Ingredients:

- ✓ 300g fresh salmon fillet
- ✓ 200g asparagus beans, trimmed
- ✓ 1 onion, chopped
- ✓ 2 garlic cloves, minced
- ✓ 3 cups low-sodium vegetable broth
- ✓ 1 cup light cream
- ✓ 1 tablespoon olive oil
- ✓ Salt and pepper to taste
- ✓ Fresh dill for garnish

Step-by-Step Preparation:

1. In a pot, heat olive oil over medium heat and sauté onion and garlic until translucent.
2. Add asparagus beans and cook for 5 minutes.
3. Pour in vegetable broth and bring to a simmer.
4. Add salmon and cook until it's easily flaked with a fork.
5. Stir in light cream, season with salt and pepper.
6. Cook for an additional 5 minutes.
7. Garnish with fresh dill before serving.

Nutritional Facts: (Per serving)

- ✓ Calories: 250
- ✓ Protein: 18g
- ✓ Fat: 15g
- ✓ Carbohydrates: 10g
- ✓ Sodium: 200mg

Creamy Soup with Salmon and Asparagus Beans is a symphony of flavors and textures, perfect for those who appreciate a gourmet touch in their meals. Whether it's a cozy dinner or a special occasion, this soup is sure to impress with its combination of simplicity, elegance, and nutritional benefits.

Chapter 07: Lean Sips & Smooth Blends

Recipe 01 : Chocolate Peanut Butter Banana

Unleash the ultimate blend of taste and nutrition with this Chocolate Peanut Butter Banana smoothie. A perfect pick for fitness enthusiasts, this low-calorie, high-protein drink combines the richness of chocolate with the creamy texture of peanut butter and the natural sweetness of banana for a delightful treat.

Servings: 2

Prepping Time: 5 minutes

Cook Time: 0 minutes

Difficulty: Easy

Ingredients:

- ✓ 1 large banana, frozen
- ✓ 2 tablespoons peanut butter
- ✓ 1 tablespoon unsweetened cocoa powder
- ✓ 1 cup unsweetened almond milk
- ✓ 1 scoop protein powder (chocolate or vanilla)
- ✓ Ice cubes (optional)

Step-by-Step Preparation:

1. Place the frozen banana, peanut butter, cocoa powder, almond milk, and protein powder in a blender.

2. Blend on high until smooth and creamy. Add ice cubes for a thicker consistency if desired.

3. Pour into glasses and serve immediately.

Nutritional Facts: (Per serving)

- ✓ Calories: 200
- ✓ Protein: 15g
- ✓ Fat: 8g
- ✓ Carbohydrates: 18g
- ✓ Fiber: 4g

Indulge in the creamy, chocolaty goodness of this Chocolate Peanut Butter Banana smoothie without any guilt. Whether you need a post-workout boost or a satisfying snack, this smoothie will hit the spot while keeping your fitness goals on track.

Recipe 02 Whey Vanilla Protein Shake

This Whey Vanilla Protein Shake is a delicious, low-calorie option for those seeking a high-protein drink. It blends smoothly, offering a refreshing taste perfect for any time of the day.

Servings: 1

Prepping Time: 5 minutes

Cook Time: 0 minutes

Difficulty: Easy

Ingredients:

- 1 scoop vanilla whey protein powder
- 1 cup unsweetened almond milk
- ½ banana, frozen
- 1 tablespoon chia seeds
- Ice cubes (optional)

Step-by-Step Preparation:

1. Place the vanilla whey protein powder, unsweetened almond milk, frozen banana, and chia seeds into a blender.
2. Add ice cubes if desired for a colder shake.
3. Blend on high until smooth and creamy.
4. Pour into a glass and serve immediately.

Nutritional Facts: (Per serving)

- Calories: 220
- Protein: 25g
- Carbohydrates: 18g
- Fat: 6g
- Fiber: 4g

This Whey Vanilla Protein Shake is a treat for your taste buds and a boost for your health. Its easy preparation and rich nutritional profile make it the perfect choice for a quick breakfast or post-workout refreshment. Enjoy the creamy, smooth texture and the benefits of high protein in every sip.

Recipe 03 : Banana Strawberry Cocktail With Cocoa

Dive into the delightful blend of flavors with our Banana Strawberry Cocktail with Cocoa, a low-calorie, high-protein masterpiece. This unique concoction combines the sweetness of fruits with the richness of cocoa, making it an ideal choice for health enthusiasts with a sweet tooth.

Servings: 2

Prepping Time: 10 minutes

Cook Time: 0 minutes

Difficulty: Easy

Ingredients:

- ✓ 1 banana, sliced
- ✓ 1 cup strawberries, fresh or frozen
- ✓ 1 tablespoon cocoa powder, unsweetened
- ✓ 1 scoop vanilla or chocolate protein powder
- ✓ 1 cup almond milk, unsweetened
- ✓ Ice cubes, optional

Step-by-Step Preparation:

1. Combine the banana, strawberries, cocoa powder, protein powder, and almond milk in a blender.

2. Add ice cubes if a colder cocktail is desired.

3. Blend until smooth and creamy.

4. Pour into glasses and serve immediately, garnished with a strawberry or banana slice if desired.

Nutritional Facts: (Per serving)

- ✓ Calories: 150
- ✓ Protein: 10g
- ✓ Carbohydrates: 23g
- ✓ Fat: 3g
- ✓ Fiber: 5g

Embrace the fusion of banana, strawberry, and cocoa in this refreshing cocktail. Perfect for a nutritious start to your day or as a post-workout treat, it's not just a drink but a healthy indulgence. Enjoy the creamy texture and rich flavors, all while fueling your body with the protein it needs.

Recipe 04 : Avocado Blueberry Smoothie Garnish

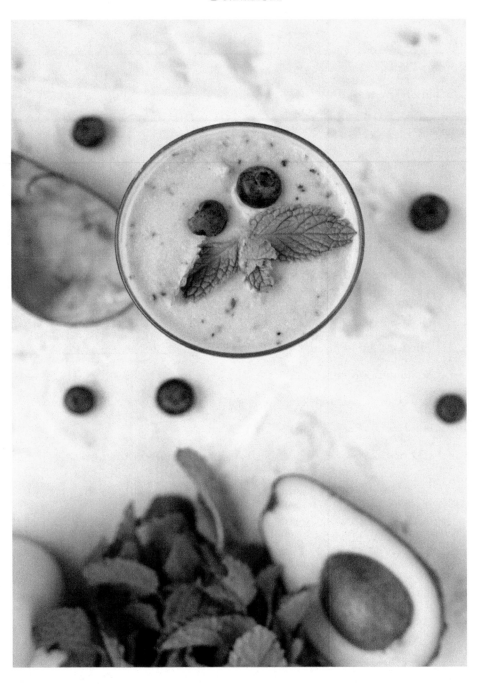

Dive into a refreshing blend of health with this Avocado Blueberry Smoothie Garnish. Perfect for a nutritious start or a mid-day boost, it combines the creamy texture of avocado with the sweet tang of blueberries, offering a delicious way to stay fit.

Servings: 2

Prepping Time: 10 minutes

Cook Time: 0 minutes

Difficulty: Easy

Ingredients:

- ✓ 1 ripe avocado, peeled and pitted
- ✓ 1 cup fresh blueberries
- ✓ 1/2 cup Greek yogurt
- ✓ 1 tablespoon honey
- ✓ 1/2 cup almond milk
- ✓ Ice cubes (optional)

Step-by-Step Preparation:

1. Combine avocado, blueberries, Greek yogurt, honey, and almond milk in a blender.
2. Add ice cubes if desired for a chilled version.
3. Blend until smooth.
4. Pour into glasses and serve immediately for the best taste and texture.

Nutritional Facts: (Per serving)

- ✓ Calories: 280
- ✓ Protein: 10g
- ✓ Fat: 15g
- ✓ Carbohydrates: 30g
- ✓ Fiber: 7g

Wrap up your day with this Avocado Blueberry Smoothie Garnish, a delightful concoction that's a feast for your taste buds and a boon for your health. Low in calories yet high in protein, it's the perfect guilt-free indulgence for anyone looking to nourish their body without compromising flavor.

Recipe 05 : Chocolate Smoothie With Banana

Embrace the blissful harmony of flavors with our Chocolate Smoothie with Banana - a perfect concoction for those who don't want to compromise on taste while keeping track of their health. This low-calorie, high-protein smoothie blends the creamy texture of banana with chocolate's rich, indulgent taste, offering a nutritious way to satisfy your cravings.

Servings: 2

Prepping Time: 5 minutes

Cook Time: 0 minutes

Difficulty: Easy

Ingredients:

- ✓ 2 ripe bananas
- ✓ 2 tablespoons cocoa powder
- ✓ 1 cup unsweetened almond milk
- ✓ 1/2 cup low-fat Greek yogurt
- ✓ 1 tablespoon maple syrup or honey (optional)
- ✓ Ice cubes (optional)

Step-by-Step Preparation:

1. Peel the bananas and cut them into chunks.
2. Combine bananas, cocoa powder, almond milk, Greek yogurt, and maple syrup or honey in a blender.
3. Add ice cubes for a colder smoothie, if desired.
4. Blend until smooth and creamy.
5. Pour into glasses and serve immediately, enjoying every sip of this guilt-free indulgence.

Nutritional Facts: (Per serving)

- ✓ Calories: 195
- ✓ Protein: 9g
- ✓ Fat: 2g
- ✓ Carbohydrates: 40g
- ✓ Fiber: 5g

This Chocolate Smoothie with Banana is more than just a treat; it's a testament that healthy eating can be delicious and satisfying. Whether you're looking for a quick breakfast, a post-workout recharge, or a sweet snack, this smoothie is a nutritious choice that won't disappoint.